In The Shadows of Eden

Written By:
Jana Alibrandi

Order this book online at www.trafford.com
or email orders@trafford.com

Most Trafford titles are also available at major online book retailers.

Printed in the United States of America.

ISBN: 978-1-4269-3662-3 (sc)
ISBN: 978-1-4269-3663-0 (e-b)

Our mission is to efficiently provide the world's finest, most comprehensive book publishing service, enabling every author to experience success. To find out how to publish your book, your way, and have it available worldwide, visit us online at www.trafford.com

Trafford rev. 07/08/2010

 www.trafford.com

North America & international
toll-free: 1 888 232 4444 (USA & Canada)
phone: 250 383 6864 ♦ fax: 812 355 4082

Book Of Poems

Written By: Jana Alibrandi

Edited By: Katie Ruggiero

TABLE OF CONTENTS

Fallen Petals in the Shadows of Eden

The walls decay in a bloody cave
Love for a century is countless in days
Lies feel longer than an eternity
Does the term loyalty apply?
Why, when all I do is share
The petal of deceit
This broken chair has had its last sway
This wooden shamble is not mine
It never really was
My heels walk better alone
Rather than sit and rock with filth
You sang your lullabies
Truth sings slowly along with a heart full of smoke
I fought for you and your bandaged lies
Now is the time to radiate with pride
The shield of love no longer resides as I put it to rest
You will never again receive my abundant gifts
My life is what I make of it
Your unwanted petal has fallen
And my womb will blossom into
A garden more pleasing than Eden!

CANDY EYES DON'T LIE

All I have is time to sit
As I grasp it
Months and years go by
Time flies by as I sit with it
Shattered to pieces
Inch by inch
I let go of it
My wounded heartfelt soul sits
Please don't share this
It is meant for only you and me
Tasteless candy sits well on a shelf
I ask only this, please don't share it
These peppermint words are for no one else to see
No copy to write
No fist fight
Just my words
And my wounded heart
As I hold it together
And answer a letter that was never even sent

BLUE SKIES

My dreams have vanished into a heap of ashes
Yet cigars and lattes calm the blues
Time is ticking and still no news to write home about
Be it as it may, I've got nothing to say
It's just another lonely day, yours truly J
I could make pretend that I danced with the rat pack
I could make pretend that I met Robert Deniro
And that he agreed to make my ideas into a film
Or I could even dream that I was an extra in a movie
A movie that won Leonardo DiCaprio an Oscar
Yet instead I'll sip a cappuccino and be happy for them

Environmental Society
Dedicated to the Youth

Do you honestly know what it is like
To walk in their shoes?
If not then be silent before you speak
About things you are unaware of
Imagine if you will a shotgun
Every damn night
When you try to do your college-prep homework
One damn class that you can't even afford
The electricity is out
But lighters and candles make good light at night
Trying to write a paper without a pen
Until you see a friend
Who makes a copy on her computer later
When youth walk by and never smile
You ask what's their problem, Damn!
You see, they just really don't have anything to smile about
You won't find dinner in a refrigerator to be reheated
A stale bag of pretzels will do
Imagine the fear as you sit in a room with three windows
Knowing drive bys are always an accidental death

Just a test, and that chip on their shoulder gets bigger and bigger
And you mention their bad attitude
When all I see is an environmental society
I smile once in a while when cops drive by my friends
Because I choose the narrow grounds
But when the lights flash on to another mission
My body feels tension, not to mention
I dropped out of that class
And probably won't go back
I kept on feeling like I was having a heart attack
But I don't think my medical covers that
When roads are paved in gold it's easy to forget
But when the blood stained streets are tagged with yellow caution tape
It's so hard to remember life without the police
Check it out before you attack it, and know it before you scold it
Write it when you've lived it!

CREATE

Deception is all I encounter
From people who have yet to understand the meaning of life
When sleeping around is present
When a hit to the face tends to replace the love
That has been lost somewhere in space
When you have been let go
But have done nothing wrong
Except following through with your creativity
The creativity that has control over your emotion
A passion that exists, but is never recognized
If I could enlighten those who have yet to appreciate life
To appreciate love for what it really is
But then again differences are what make the world go round
And all things happen for a reason
So I take it in stride
Until a higher being enlightens me to be who I am
With love to give, with a life to live, and with the passion of creativity
The passion that will never leave this strained mind
Because creativity is the only real love of mine

CULTURE

These cities around me
Where not an inch of culture lies
To die
In the midst of Malden how profound no culture
Except for the spot I lay my pen
No one is talking
No thoughts to transcend
Memories of lost friends
I guess every place has a home where you can lay your misery
Does destiny lie beyond this hole of a city
Or shall I stay and become the culture it needs
Besides this bar, not a youngster in this place
Not a character to taste
Dullness, what a disgrace
So I stay and manipulate a way to bring you a little culture
To those of you who have something to bring
Let it be
You are a part of the culture I've been dying to see

AFFLUENT WOMAN

She is graceful and prestigious, so many adore her
She listens to the pain and grief of others
And may even shed a tear
Something we call emotion
And when it seems time for a blessing she may
Even speak to the man upstairs for only their sake
Putting herself last, just a sacrifice
She puts down the swords so many men carry
She releases energy others can't explain
Tempted by vision but never thrown back
If something is troubled
She steps forth to keep it intact
And for the only one she attracts is forever in her heart
She is a symbol of peace throughout the wars ahead
She wipes the tears
Calms the shakes
And holds the torch of endorsing fate
Only if there were more men like her

A Little Bit of This, A Little Bit of That
Inspired by the movie Good Will Hunting

Talent this
Talent that
What about the depth that lies underneath his hat
Don't care for your schooling
Just your knowledge
Don't care for your degree
Just your wisdom
The wisdom that lies beneath your shaggy hair
Lust this
Lust that
What about the passion that lies underneath the fat
That tattered shirt
Those tattooed arms
Those spotted corduroys
This smile I see brightens my cheeks, flush as a plum
Crazy this
Crazy that
They say we are for following our dreams
Maybe I am in a sense, I know I was at one point
But you bring me reality, true sanity, and hope
Hope that I will never return to a place that lies pain
You ask how I feel and I deny what it is that I am scared of
To be abandoned that is
Love this
Love that

UNWANTED FAN

Knowing why you bought this book
Knowing why you crave attention
Knowing your selfish soul has yet to experience the beauty of love
untouched
As you leave me sick and frail
Alone in a bed
Awake I cry
Alone I stand
Knowing why you purchased this book
Oh would I mention?
Oh would she mention me?
I wouldn't give you the satisfaction
Your grease seth has yet to seep into my veins
Walking away from your ignorance
Walking away
Like you've become accustomed to when happiness wasn't a friend of
mine
I'll give you the benefit of the doubt
Maybe you will find true meaning in a higher light Someday, sometime,
some life
You're a selfish pig

I know why you bought this book, and I won't even mention your disgust of a name
As you turn the page
You can see the deeper side of me
So go ahead and judge me
Just like you have always have
Put me down for my honest emotion
Like you always will
As I ignore you for life
Knowing I possess the talent to write
Remember, I know why you bought this book
And I would never give you the satisfaction of mentioning your name

Unique

I live a life of so many identities
For my comrades
I am amusing and intractable
For my foreman
I am pure and frail
For my kin
I am strong and wise
And for my flame
I am a maiden who is yearned
The life I live has so many various identities
But to identify with myself as being unique is the key
Turn it and watch me unfold into the tapestry of gratitude
Gracious stars set far away brighten my night
Lights of loyal devotion set me apart from weak mammals
As I drabble in my lioness mane
And for my flame, I am yearned

HIP TO THE GAME
Dedicated to local Boston Hip Hop Artists

Narrow-minded people need to get hip to the game
The punk ass wanna-be gangsters that lie
About the bank they wish they held up
Feel no emotion for anyone because they are tough
Get hip to the game, it's positive over negative
You know the ones who rap about how many men they've shot
And for a woman they would never tie the knot
Except for Mary Jane, gotta smoke that pot
Wake up, it's positive over negative
When that man brags about how many times he's hit it in a week
When in reality he's never even snuck a peek
Get a grip, because it's positive over negative
When someone insists they are open-minded
But in reality they have closed the door on life
Snap out of it, it's positive over negative
When psychiatrists insist people are crazy
When in reality they are just fun
Crack down, it's positive over negative
When people discourage you because you're different
Be positive, influence your perception
Because people need to wake up, snap out,
Get a grip and get hip to the game

DEVOTED MAID

When I was a child, crayons and paper
Were always put back in their original spot
Moving on to adult hood
Yeah I was there when he denied his child
I was there on that cold November day
I held her when he took her purity and stomped all over her pulsating
heart
I humored you when your educated guess wasn't too sharp
I recited the joke and deaf men laughed
I was there when he was on probation
Sacrificing last chances to see old friends
To be with you homeward bound
And you, yeah you
Do you remember me picking up the mess?
Holding you as you shook
A friendly date
Taking you to rehab, acupuncture at its best
Poems to refresh
Now do you remember me picking up the mess?
Cokehead friends slowly undress
Haunting them with my presence
Speaking the truth as they live lies
Not him, the dirty whore they deceived
But me, the pest

Eventually my premonitions come into effect
Now do you remember me picking up the mess?
Oh and I'm not quite done
You over there pretending nothing's wrong
Homeless you were, and in tune so was I
Do you remember that cold cement floor where I often accompanied you?
Do you remember the nights we slept in my car?
Do you remember the sixteen hundred dollars I put down on that apartment?
Yeah the one you scared off with a violent mop
Whatever, just a test
Just me picking up the mess
Once again a child needs me, and I'm there
Fallen through the system's cracks
This time there are no take backs
A child's cries will not go unnoticed
Not in my eyes
I must confess sometimes I don't mind picking up the mess

PISSA CALL

You know what, I'm sick of this shit
Call, call, call and whine about how you want me back
No thanks!
As you walk hand in hand with a plastic imitation of me
Call, call, call and say we're just friends
Don't care, don't explain, don't lie the evident lie again
Just go away
Call, call, call
Will you please see me on my birthday?
But only as friends okay?
Never seen, don't care
But still I receive that damn call once again
I changed my number
I've changed my life
Now will you be with me?
Well I've changed too
Now I've got that super repellent mighty might
Don't mess with me anymore
You're like a disease that never heals, and for some odd reason I loved
you
Pissa huh?

Wish I could turn back the hands of time
And judge you like I should have
You are a piece of scum, due to your environment
But it's not up to me anymore to help sooth it
So you can make like a tree and leave
Go take a long walk off a short pier
I don't care how you do it, just do it like Nike™ says
Call after call, you wish you were never born
Ironic, so do I
Yeah, I guess I'm a bitch
Yeah, well you take what they inflict and you see where you stand
Rain on my head, dog shit in my hand
Real pissa huh?

ECSTASY
Inspired by the band "Rusted Root"

Walk on by
Living in a world of ecstasy
Walk on by
To a new society
In it there shall be
Work for free
As long as we all agree
Living in a world of ecstasy
Teach the truth
Behind the lies
Express your flesh
No disguise
If you choose
Free will to be what it is that you are
If you haven't found it
Follow and you shall find
Power of the mind
Living in ecstasy

HARVARD'S EXTENSION

Bloody distractions have revolutionized my writing
A father's intention is greater
Than a volcano erupting in the stillness of Hawaii
Burgundy wine has an accentuated taste
When it lifts one's spirits
As does the eighty percent chance that determines his son's life extension
Words flow for my courses red corrections while excessive vials are drawn
Bone marrow is no longer an illusion with injections of sweet scientific magic
In tune, an intelligent child who's knowledge is remarkable
Will live to see another year
Questioning my fatigued nervousness to be the best
A writer with remarkable status
Regardless, lessons are learned when blood-marked papers are returned

DUMBFOUND

They all let me down
Shhh…Hush
Not a sound
Don't say you're sorry
Don't say you care
Don't say you miss me
Cause you probably don't anyway
No one really does
I'm lost without love
Lost without the ones who have vanished
No soft kiss that means the world
No call to see if I'm okay
You all remain far away
Hush, as you leave
And when you were here, something still wasn't there
Something missing
My friends, do they know I care?
My brother, who I love deeply
My love, that never really was all there
They leave, is it me?
Do I project evil?
The evil they portray to be okay
Hush, I shut down my tone
For the love has grown ever since you've been missing

Missing from the fears
Missing from the tears
From the lies, missing
Does anyone respond to my saddened eyes?
I hear no replies
Hello, is anyone there? If so, can you hear me?
It taunts me, as they remain silent water fills my pupils
Can you read into my disgust
As I cuss, and break you?
Hurt you, desert you, I don't hear you
Do I piss you off?
Do I strike your mind every now and then
Or do I blend in to the thought's subconscious?
As I let go, as I wait
No one speaks, nor do I
Shhh…Hush…
That's all that is said
That's all I dread
As silence lurks
What would you like me to do?
Portray me as your fool
Let you stay dumb
Speak! For God's sake speak!
Someone ease the pain
Someone let me feel again
Speak! Because God knows I will remain dumb

Karma Enforcer
Inspired by the song "Karma Police" by Radiohead
Dedicated to Ruby

As we lie awake
Your confused tactics
The rapist does exist
Rape people of their pride
Rape people of their self worth
Who me? Never
Get hip to the game
You must give in order to receive
True karma does exist in this universe
The universe you perceive as your own
But I see through your inner soul
True karma will proceed into the depths of despair you've made others
feel
And in tune, the rapist yearns for a love that is real
You are a human being in disguise
So many identities, yet haven't found the one worth leaving the addiction
for
Addicted to theft
Addicted to lies

Addicted to me, that drug that gives you a high
An unbelievable high you have yet to encounter
Because my love is higher lifting
More than heroin, more than cocaine,
More than a rapist can handle
You can't handle the real Italian ice that is yet to be broken
Besides, this karma will intervene, with the desire longing to find peace
So take it as a token
Karma does exist

OPEN MIC

TJ's Bar and Grille gave us locals a place to control
This structure held us together like no other in an overzealous town
Underneath the stench of stale cigarette breath
Lies the uplifting conversations and manifestations of souls that will always mesh
Diverse, yet unified groups trying to make a change in the midst of alcoholic beverages
The dim lights made it easy to see an array of real people's persona
Miraculous, harmonic endeavors we thought we would never overcome
At last, the captivating sound of guitars strummed
The beat of the bongo drum
While voices chanted, "Jana Speak To Me"
The sound flowed like swans gliding along a pond only meant for them
Words echoed through the attentive soldiers hearts, marking a revelation
On the contrary, science had its role while chemistry problem solutions were laid out
On fresh napkins with Keno pencils
Not to mention the sweet carousel of a poet's dream
And what they all mean with the deepest sincerity

Embracing variation with our peers left a permanent impression
Unfortunately, this cathedral of hope vanished late spring two years ago
And our resting home is now a bare, empty, desolate parking lot
Although we have disbursed and declined our throne
Conformed to rent uncontrolled
Cherishing our memories and motivating passions will always be significant
Even in the stillness of our separate, solemn-appointed quarters

ALIENS

Does anyone know I'm here, in the corner of my bed with a cigarette?
A book of matches, a pen and some words, I'd rather speak than write
But no one's here to listen to the words tonight
Aliens, enemies
Aliens, friends
Loves that last, okay, they never do
He's sick with Aids, yeah well I got the flu
You date and live with a Nazi, well I sometimes chill with this kid who's
a Jew
You say you're pregnant, so what, if I wanted to I could be too
What's that? Your girl never calls?
That's funny, my ex prank called me the other night
What's that? You hate me? I'm a bitch? That's cool
Maybe I'll see you tomorrow before school
You're an addict, can't handle the withdrawal
By the way, this kid said he banged me, but I don't recall
Aliens, enemies
Aliens, friends
Humina? A vampire is poisoning you in your dreams?
That reminds me, aliens like the color green

Oh, you think you're gay? Well I bit my tongue the other day
Wait a minute! This kid is telling me back in New York he got shot in
the leg
Well I once got pushed by this girl named Meg
Wait, did you say you missed me? No, you just give good head
I don't, but I'm still sitting in my bed waiting for a call, a shout, or even
a moving mouth
But all I get is the sound of my head rambling on
I cry for no reason
I cry for world peace
We live in an ongoing institution
Coping with society to find a solution
Can you relate?
Sorry, you were saying? Oh, tonight's your first date?
Interesting
Aliens, enemies
Aliens, friends
Humans, strange
Humans change

YEARNING A FIT NECKLACE
Dedicated to the Single Mothers

The necklace is torn, who will give birth to my newborn?
Chakra speak to me in rapid sound
As he penetrates me we are granted pound
Inch by inch I receive him, I think he's okay for now
But a father he has yet to consume
As the plot thickens, for it feels great
A sensation from within, an explosion inside my womb
As I smoke, thoughts transpire
Is this the man of my dreams?
If not, does he exist?
I travel from a virgin with much respect
To a prostitute with yet another regret
I should have remained pure for that good old Mr. Right
But then again, he might have complained that I was too tight
I have given up on finding one true soul in which to cling
For he has yet to find me
Release that pain

Let's set sail, yes, the female must set sail
Don't stop for fish or water
Track only until you explore your island of gifts
That allow your presence to shine
Then the two souls will intertwine into enormous triumph
And if a chill wind blows later that evening
And you catch the distant fever
Remember, you are still an angel's little diva

Sometimes Silver is Better than Gold

He brings me roses of gold, but I like silver
I said he brings me flowers of gold, but I like silver
He brushes my hair, smooth and straight
But I like it wild and kinky
He buys me new shoes, black leather with a thick pump
But all I want is to walk barefoot through some good, old-fashioned funk
He hands me twenty-four grand to pursue an education
When all I want is a penny to make a wish
He tempts me with heroin and cocaine
But a cup of java and a cigarette will do
He wants to fill my head with Nazi thoughts, but my best friend is Jewish
He wants me to hate gays, but I don't even though
That's not how society is being raised
He wants me to come along for a night of pleasure
As he beats a black man on the corner
Little does he know, that he is our ancestor
He makes comments that Asians can't drive
Little does he know that it's my nephew inside
He laughs at the disturbed and lights them on fire
Little does he know I'm in flames as we speak

He is narrow-minded, I am not
That's why this relationship has come to a stop
Now he doesn't bring me gold roses anymore
Because he knows I like silver
I said he doesn't bring me gold roses anymore
Because he knows I like silver
But right about now, I'd rather have bronze

COME HOME

There is so much around me
I need to do what's best for me
I need to strive in the right direction
I need to be well known for my talents
I need to be loved due to fate
The ones I love are worlds away
The ones that are close in miles are far away in depth
Relating to you is all that's left to fill this space
Ones in search of a dream
While others are in search of an education
And some others are in search of meaning
Come home
Come home to the boredom
Come home to the dull
Come home to me
The ones who love you the most
Come home before I break without you
Come home and we can start our project
Come home and we can grow into the vision I have for us
Come home and be successful
Come home and live with me, it's our destiny
Come home to a kiss
Come home to a hug
Come home to me
Come home to love

COLORADO SHOOTING

Homicide, attention!
Suicide, nothing
I hear nothing
Children suffer from depression
Children tease
Killers suffer from taunting remarks
Change your outlook
Sickness in their veins
As others repel it
Destiny awaits, and if I shall die
You, the one who has inflicted my illness, shall cease as well
A lesson is to be taught
Recognized for who we are
We are told to be bold
Stop the pain
Stop the lies
Stop the suicide
Before it escalates to homicide

In the Mist of Heat
Inspired by my local tanning salon

As I lay in this bed of heat
Rays penetrate my soul
Relaxation from within
All frustration is released
As sweat pours down my chin
Sensations, thoughts of my many men
I hear the beat as it thumps harder
No cares for the neck, less I wear
The line will not interfere
Now the beat softens, as does the light of warmth
I feel at ease, until I leave
And return to the blessed mess
But granted, I am darker

Sandy Highlights

I feel for her, although she is not my friend
She stares through a plate of glass, what is she wondering?
Why does she seem so displeased?
She asks questions that are so simple, like my hair tone and style
Wishing she had the same
Something is missing from her life
And it's not my sandy highlights
It's exposure
Exposed to the real world
Life as we know it
Each evening, I glance to see her staring through a plate of glass
Into the world of the unknown
She wishes she were somewhere else in time
Now I realize she is no different from me
I sometimes wish I could be there
On top of the world, reaching my goals and dreams
Although she is not known, she is not a stranger

PRETTY IN WHITE

She looks pretty in white, I overheard him say
She will make him a beautiful wife someday
I look into her adult eyes, and see her childish fun
Remembrance of the titter tat
Old friends that chat
I overheard him say
I almost had her close to my heart
Buy I chose to push her away
I overheard him say
She loves that spring, and she once loved me
Yet I chose to push her away
I see her dance with a gracious touch
Everything about her trembles in my clutch
I miss her so much
She looks pretty in white, I overheard him say
I'll make him a beautiful wife someday

Tapped
Dedicated to the pre-teen girls

I'm not as pretty as I'd like to be
I'm not as thin as I used to be
But you say I'm the one you adore
My eyes shine like the stars
It's true you said you loved me a little too soon
I'm not a fool, I have never been tapped
For I am still pure
And now I know that's all you're looking for
To peek inside of me
My only soul, well I leave it up to me
For I will not burst into the creature who hunts me
I will run and hide away from this temptation
The evil temptation that creeps
Because I know the true beauty lies inside of me

MYSTICAL SOULS

Break through the chains
Break through the conformity
My mate's soul shall not escape and sizzle into leftover vegetation
Determination
Your heart oozes with unknown blood
Must flee into the capacity where hearts are lifted
Let your star shine
We are each other's sparkling wish that lifts higher and flows with
energy
Oh, for Buddha's sake, let our star shine, and maybe intertwine into
both swan
He and she
Insight strikes me to ease the fear
For souls enlightened are aware
We stand in glassed in an oval tear
Courage to speak
As the words mutter in disguise, out of our mouths and into each other's
eyes
Intrigued by the mind

Courage, I see a spider
Courage, I draw a feather
The courage to stare
The courage to state the glare
The sake, for take, taboo, who knew?
Beneath me, never
Beside me, clever
Soul mate, forever

SOMETHING'S BREWING

I travel to meet with a friend, yet you drove by at five a.m.
I picked up a pack of cigarettes at an all night store
But you drove by at four and waited, you waited at my door
I dismissed a fight that started off right and ended a mess
While you drove by at three o'clock, pest
I sipped a few with you and some others
Danced to a song and met with friends, while you left at two a.m.
Where did you think I went?
Of course you care
But I've got something brewing upstairs
I've got something that's pleasing so far
So why do you constantly drive by in your car?
If you need to speak your piece then by all means do
If you're silent, screw!
I've got plans to brew, meeting someone and moving forth
Distant love is just a smirk
It will be okay, you're fine without me
I just cause stress, besides you hate the way I dress
Ha! Did I make you laugh? Did I make you smile?
No! You just sit there in denial
Come on, we've been friends for a while
You don't love me, I'll tell you again, so don't think that you do
Don't misinterpret the lines that you threw
Don't think lightly, just think with your head

Some things are better off unsaid
You don't love me, yeah see I've said it again
Distant sorrow, distant regret, you'll transcend
Hearts mend, memories fade
So why did you drive by early on Sunday?
With nothing to lose, sorry you said you loved me a little too soon
Ah, a little too late but at any rate
I've got plans to brew
I've got places to go, American quilts to sew
Lives to save, visits to graves
More importantly, poems to write
Sorry, do I sound too uptight?
Besides the tears, how was your night?
I'm sorry I hurt you but it's for the best
It wouldn't have worked in the end, I know
It's okay, just let go
Trust me it's for the best
And your puppy brown eyes ask
As you left, I closed the door behind you and wrote this piece
I know it's not a love song or a well thought out sonnet
But for some reason I just can't get on it
You see I've got plans to brew
I'm stirring them as we speak
I feel special and unique
And no one's going to take that away from me!

GLIDE ON SMOOTH

Glide on smooth
Clear sky night
Glitter summer lake
In a down and out canoe
Is even more soothing than a yacht filled with caviar in their broad
ocean
Look off into the sunset
What is meant, is meant to be
Awaiting a lifetime of change
Awaiting a job to advance
It seems my life has passed me by
Wondering why I have chosen my paths
So suitable
Yet poets' dreams travel in their souls
No matter what distances they go
Filled with life, not a hollow shell in sight
Bye-bye my cherry bloom
For now, I will visit again soon
While we sail on so smooth

Where is My Home?
Dedicated to the Beantown Boys

Eastie was always tough
But back then you had Beantown fighters
Loyal to the bone unless you mess with their home
Forget it!
You can imagine the beating
Beantown thrown
As an adult, I can't seem to provide a safe home
Finances are a struggle
And the neighborhood is trouble
Where there used to be burgers on the grill and late night chatter
Instead there are the mad hatters
Those foreign faces with bandanas
Color codes and abbreviations
Stalking as you walk by on a Sunday afternoon
Clearly it can't be that bad, this is my city!
Late one night coming in after visiting old friends
I smile at the thought of their presence
Enter my home and place my silver pocketbook on the kitchen chair
Enter my bathroom to wash up for the night
I hear Bang! Bang! Six times!
Who am I kidding nothing's fine in my city
My home

THE STREETS
*Dedicated to the local police and firefighters, who
risk their lives every single day*

Walk on by as the beat thumps harder
Discourage those who want to come at you
Watch us as we tackle the wannabe phenomena
Watch your shirt as they disperse
We are superior to your wannabe gangster
Get along gangs are all the same until they are tamed
By red, white, and blue
I thought you knew how we do!
United crews blast on through and defeat you
Good luck with your father searching
It's not an excuse
Good luck with your mom pill popping jewels
News flash, it's up to you
Break the chain or be cuffed in one
Many have had it worse
Man up and play where it's tough
To be real, to be true, to be you!
Not what they need you to be, in order to feel some security
Punks follow
Lions lead with loyalty and truth
It's up to you!
No hate, just concern
The lessons you learn are greater behind bars

Papa Always Said

Sometimes the grass is not greener on the other side
Remember to always maintain your pride
Die before you lie
Remain loyal at all times
State the claims and collect your remains
Humble with fame
Take time to walk down memory lane
Stand tall
Remember who you are, as well as who you were
Remember where you're from
And how far you've come
The people who laid the tracks that way
The ones who remember your soft touch
The ones that instill confidence
You know who they are
And they know you all to well

SOMETHING'S GOING DOWN
From the Book Mystical Souls

Out for the night with an old friend
Known since I was fourteen
Drinking and dancing with a couple who are digging on us
Another friend enters the scene with their Celtic cross in flames
Reciting how there's gonna be a fight
Not liking his thick eyebrows or his heroin ways
That my friend must be up to no good
I reply, you misunderstood
I've been by his side at all times
We're just friends, nothing's going down
The Mick leaves knowing I don't want to see a fight
Considering he clawed someone who called me a name the other
night
The next encounter proceeds
As I meet with an old greaser friend and cuddle until two a.m.
Mentioning the Mick was uptight
"No it's not you, it's the other kid he wants to fight"
I assure him nothing's going down
Smoke a cigarette, and a quick kiss goodbye
A brown car proceeds to follow me home

Sunday falls, I receive a few calls
One from a friend, yeah the greaser
We always meet on Sundays, eat, laugh, and chuckle
Scratch and cuddle
I fear as I leave someone is watching me
A white car, as lights shine
Yet this time they don't follow me, they haunt me
I still insist nothing's going down
Guy friends, that's that!
I don't mix and match, protectors from every end
I never bend, but somehow I sense that something's going down

THE CODMANS

My family of blood I will never forget
They have suffered, cried, and survived beside me
And to my family of friends, I remember the comfort you gave me
But there is one family I left behind in a sense
The Codman family comes to mind every now and then
The Codmans lived in a log cabin surrounded by woods
Where I was found in desperate need of help
I sustained the winter snow trapped in a ditch
Until the Codmans found me and nursed me back to health
They read me a story about a Native American princess
They stroked my hair ever so gently until I fell fast asleep
They drew pictures of the first creatures to ever roam the Earth
And in this moment I was given the precious gift of life
And when I left on that warm summer's day, I was better but still not
my best
I had received so much, but had not given anything back in return

That is why I returned two years later
To find that warm woodsy cabin abandoned
With no trace of the family that I had left behind
The closest I came was to a woman riding on a tall white horse
She spoke vaguely of them when I mentioned how kind they were to me
This came as a surprise, for they were amazing people
She laughed as if I was strange for knowing them
Then her horse arched back and tumbled over
The gifts that I had brought for them
Although I am unable to give my gifts to the Codmans
I know whenever there is someone that is ill and in need
I can give them what I have received

HOPE FOR THE UNSEEN

The truth of the millennium
Those who haven't shall
Those who have suffered shall receive
Those who deceive shall retrieve
God will shun down, and those who don't will now believe
God is soft spoken, the deaf will hear his token
The blind shall see what enables thee
The dumb will speak, vibrant and true
For whatever reason that God enables you
You are blessed, to surrender and regress
Evil is the test
Don't stray, progress
Lie awake, awaken to the new horizon
The new defeat
Sun streak, moonlight high
Don't let Mother Mary cry

VOICE
Dedicated to the memory of Tommy Moschella

Speak to me, the voice that draws me in
It's subtle yet soothing, oh God I adore it
Show me the way into your heart
Because your sound has captured me
And put me in a trance
I yearn to hear your call
Mellowness takes over my soul
As I enter that trance
That sound has taken over my soul
I have seen the miracles that you can perform
I wait for the day you speak to me
And take me to your home
Many of my friends have been taken away
And I know you watch over them
You are a saint, so profound
I sing your praise, and thank you for showing me the light
I am here for a reason
Your graciousness has allowed me to live this far
But when my time comes, and I hear your subtle voice
I know you will teach me the things I have yet to learn

ITALIAN WIDOW

I've lived my life
I've been a devoted wife
Even a concerned and nurturing mother
Pans clang and clatter, tomato sauce splatter, and meatballs are rolled
For centuries, just like the ones before me
A heritage is a legacy
A heart is our family
The day my devoted soul passed
A memory, to last
For I shall put on my black shoes, skirt, and coat, all black
For centuries, just like the ones before me
A heritage is a legacy
A heart is our family
I will smile when my grandchild smiles, or says something witty
I will pray for those who are needy
I will now devote myself to prayer
And my husband's physical self that is not there
Yet I think of him in the morning light
And on cold and lonely nights
I pray for his good height

Just after I kick off my black shoes
And place them underneath our bed
Just the way he liked it
I hang my pulled, charcoal colored sweater right next to his
And lay on my side of our cushioned bed
As I've done for years
Alone I wipe away the tears
And pray for sleep, deep sleep
Peaceful, scented, angelic sleep
Nannies to the almighty kingdom
And yet I am woken by the sunlight
And I begin my cluttered day once again
Where smiles are shown
And Saints are known
Where stories are told, and meatballs are rolled
For centuries, just like the ones before me
A heritage is a legacy
A heart is our family

ALLELUIA

A day where I sit up right
In my childhood room
I hear the birds chirping
From three connected windows
I hear the voices of my seeds below
Humor, laughter, and smiles
This will always be my resting place
Yet this little bird must soar soon
Soar into a grateful man's wings
Where life is filled with ease
Love blossoms so the young flower can bloom
Different structures, yet under the same moon
I lay my pen once again, in this memory filled room
Maybe in my thoughts or in my pleasing dreams
I envision tourists interested in knowing me
Maybe a tour guide would show this colored, cluttered, clashing room
And maybe, just maybe, if my journey takes me far enough
They will say how nice I can be, and how creative I am
How much I love to laugh and to smile
But alas, this is just a dream
One worth having
One worth writing
In my cushioned tree

IT'S IN THE JOURNEY
Inspired by a conversation that took place in Cambridge, MA

I walk so slowly
Yet I always reach my destination
Take your time
Then you will enjoy the sights around you
Until you find that peaceful place
Where you can be alive
Because it's in the journey
Not the destination
We are destined for right now
Not always and forever
And if by chance that peaceful place remains calm, pure, and
beautiful
Then stay and breathe in the fresh air
But if by chance you glace and see another scene you adore just the
same, or even more
Pack up and travel
For your journey has just begun

NORTH SIDE
Dedicated to the charm of the North End of Boston
North side

Off to the North side for a drink
Not just one, more like a few
But it's okay because down here the men take care of you
With a light of your smoke, a smile, a joke
A hug and a kiss to let you know you still exist
Get up and let the lady sit, it's all good
Just one of the guys, but a lady still
Women leave, but they don't follow
We stay, their buddy
Their girl, a friend
So I remain pure and untouched
We kiss and embrace with our goodbyes
Underneath lies the truth
My man at home who works in a business suit
Not of the Italian race
Missing him often, but not when I'm at this place
I feel so at home here, with such good friends
Not worrying about traumatic ends
For the ladies missing romance, take a chance
Follow your heart, where the Italian men reside
In the North Side

Passive Prayer

You love me when I am swayed, by chance, in the wrong direction
You give me another chance to prove my love for you
You accept my thoughts of diversity and my extrovert ways
To incorporate fellow friends into my life
You always take my emotions into consideration
As I grow, so does our relationship
You embrace my physical self with a touch of love
When I feel lost and alone
All I have to do is call out your name
My calloused and scarred feet are disgusting to some
But you see the beauty of where I have been
And how I still stand tall through it all
You and your friends, you produce
And set superior meaning throughout my life
Thank you for shedding some light when I struggle
And in times of darkness
Amen

BETTER

Better to have walked among those who have stumbled
Than among those who have stood still
Better to have put yourself in a place that suffers
Than in a place that only wants
To do good amongst the less privileged
To help along those in need
It can be painful and extremely difficult to transpire with goodness
Yet you have lived trying
We are only human
But to remain in an island of hope and solitude would only benefit one's
self
Why dwell with the hopeless while striving to help them find peace
Better to have taught savages and know they have learned well
Than to dance with the proper who have failed
Better to be humble within yourself than to be proud among others
Better to be myself than any other
Better to drink water with those who have loved
Than to drink wine with those who have killed
Better to write than to date

Better to sleep than to toss and turn all night
Better to be sad for one moment in time
Than to pretend joy for an eternity
Better to be wrong and to have learned from experience
Than to have never learned at all
As I sit I am better to have been than to have not
Yes, as I sit I am better to have been than to have not

DELICATE KISS

Your distinguished smile
In which to see I would travel miles
Your soft hands touch my face
But still we have yet to embrace
As words flow out of our mouths and into each other
I gasp, and hope that your lips will soon feel mine
But you resist, just waiting for the right time
And when the time comes, we merge our lips into sweet subtle flairs
I do not put up a fight
You stroke my hair ever so gently
So I preach the good word
Something about me you say you adore
If I could only lure you away in times of tears
To a place where there lie no fears, just hope for a brighter day
And I wish I could stay, but I must leave
In order to let you explore your surroundings
I relate to your saddened eyes
I seek truth underneath those lies
Our gaze is so strong, like beams of white light surrounding our aura
Eventually the words float to the tops of our throats

We slowly move closer into each other's space
Yes, our lips meet and feelings erupt in a passionate embrace
It's so strange how we met, but yet it lingers on, these feelings so strong
Wishing you were here
Sweeping my brow until I fall fast asleep
Wishing you were here
Kissing my worries away

DRAWN

Your half Asian eyes look at me with such meaning and wisdom
As I tread through crystal clear water
Preaching words of religion and belief
Chant and you shall receive
Your immense lips speak in rhythmic volume
As I smell your scent and it rises to the heavens, where God does
shine
The dreadlocks hang long for the ones who worship the black star
There is a star that proceeds clockwise, and on it they lie
His twelve disciples
Leo, Cancer, Gemini, Pisces, Aquarius
Scorpio, Capricorn, Virgo, Sagittarius
Taurus, Aries, and Libra, all follow his lead
Without them where would we be?
Your pale skin brightens the dark days, as we kneel and pray
Seeing isn't always believing, but faith is belief
No matter how it's drawn
That sacred Madonna, praised to one
Quan Yen so glorious to another

It doesn't matter how it's drawn
As long as you believe, nothing will go wrong
Nothing you can't handle that is
But no matter how it's drawn
The mystery unfolds, it is faith
It's what keeps the world going strong

DETACHED

Imagine if you will
Me in your arms
Noticing you as you walk in strongly
Noticing you as you leave softly
Your vibrant eyes show signs of low self esteem
But that doesn't bother me
Noticing those monstrous hands as they grip your last drink
And that broad chest as you stand there so still
Your lips, oh those lips, luscious yet subtle
Talking in ways I can understand
Noticing you laugh as you converse
Noticing your smile
I'm here, here in the corner
A light shines over me
I'm here expressing my extrovert ways
I'm here with determination on my face
I'm here, here in the corner
Does anyone notice me the way I notice you?

RELEASE

Have you ever loved someone
But refused to let them know?
Because I have
As the days, months, and years pass by
I wonder why I choose to remain silent
Maybe I'm afraid to make a move
But when I finally get the courage to tell you what I'm feeling
You come to me with a situation
A situation that involves the woman you love
I hold in the heartbreak and release advice
I hold back the tears and release a smile
If you only knew
I would do all the things that your woman won't do
Now you realize that I am your lover
So you hold me and whisper sincere words of love
When the sun goes down and my eyelids are closed
It feels real and true but we all must awaken
And so I return to being your blessed friend
A friendship that will last
A friendship that will hurt

THE LEGEND
Inspired by Frank Sinatra, a true legend

My love for you is eternal
Although we are strangers in the morning, day, and night
You bring me up into the highest light
When my soul is alone and shady
I'm on lockdown, even though you're so far away
But that's life I struggle with day to day
If I had the chance to meet I would probably say
Something stupid, like I love you
Cause you did it your way
The light of your cigarette, your tilted hat
As you leave me softly
Forget about the golden arm, you lived a golden life
And this year when the summer wind comes rolling in
We will stroll along and sing your song
Because in this town, your legend lives on

Spirits We Lift

Winter seasons flow
With intoxication on our breath
Family, friends, and fun is exhaled
Love of the spirits we lift, my angels and me
Foreign voices consumed by static
Waiting for my next tactic
Kiss me, sweet
Argue, strong
Agree, pleasantly
Finally nothing bothers me
Wait, I receive a call and hear breathing on the other end
I sit an await the joy of my friends' arrival
I look off into the distance, at a shadow of a man I once thought I
knew
Tragic lovers that grew apart
Some say a blessing in disguise
Soft spoken lies, playing the roles I adore
Truth proceeds, location leaves
Finally nothing bothers me
Past remembrances, of a domestic dispute
Loss of loot
Stalker ways, but it's okay I'm safe
With my angels at my side, finally nothing bothers me

Inevitable
Inspired by the Shores of Cape Cod in Massachusetts

A lobster nips at my toe
A whale swallows me whole
It's inevitable
A statue sits on a rock, watching the waves crash in
The sun enlightens me as its beams penetrate my soul
Lost without the fame
Lost without the glory
It's inevitable
Traveling far to meet his performance
And in return I am granted distance
My good luck charm, he has broken down without me
I am hoping he finds fulfillment in his journey
But you must not mistake beauty for love
It's inevitable
Reaching out to someone who hasn't the time
Reaching out to someone who hasn't found meaning
Reaching out to you, the one I am so proud of
It's inevitable

Ciao Bella

Buon giorno
Venga Qui!
Bello
The sun mesmerizes my soul
As it shines wherever I am
It leads me in the right direction
And no matter how hard I fall
It pulls me up into a higher light
A higher energy that only I can feel
It inspires me to write words of such meaning
The generation will transpire into the obvious
The tradition lives on
Buona sera!
Ciao bella!

STRENGTH

I've reached my highest point
I will even create once again
I am climbing the ladder of fame
Whether I stand tall
Or break and fall
I will always be your friend
Some bonds are just a trend
But for myself everlasting
Some bonds remain strong
Others blend into the memories
That we never seem to touch base on
I struggle like a fish without water
I struggle like a tree without sunlight
And despite this I grow
I grow into the strongest creature known to mankind
Without time for him
Without time for them
I am even stronger